THE SNAKE WITCH PLANNER

2021

Nico Harlakenden

Newton
PRESS

For information contact:
Newton Press @NewtonPressBks
www.thenewtonpress.com
Nico Harlakenden @NicoHarlakenden

Book and Cover design by Nico Harlakenden
Book Formatting by Newton Press
ISBN: 978-1-0879-1288-2

First Edition: September 2020

10 9 8 7 6 5 4 3 2 1

CONTENTS

Introduction

The Snake as Wisdom

THE FIRST THING YOU THINK OF when someone says the word 'snake' might be a slithering cold-blooded reptile. It might be the seducer in the biblical garden of paradise. The word may even conjure thoughts of the Devil himself. Would it surprise you to find out much of history has held a different and complex view of this creature?

The snake has been associated with creation, wisdom, and magic since before recorded history. We'll touch upon some of the more fascinating historical examples later in this book, but to clear up any misconceptions I'd like to make it clear that this is not a religious text. I don't believe that witchcraft has anything to do with any classification of God, gods, or goddesses. If your personal path has brought you to a crossroad (pun intended) where you do experience an overlap of the sacred and the profane I hold no judgement.

As a practice there is not meant to be any barrier to entry. This archetype of snake as bearer of wisdom is older than the written word. There is no language, geographic, religious, or cultural limitation to the following associations or divinitory traditions. That is part of what I find so intriguing about them.

Rather than being a devotional to deities this book is about the now-arcane tradition of marrying the mantic and the sophic -- of combining the faculty of divination with developed wisdom. When we give ourselves space to reflect on our intuitions and observations, our experiences become richer, we embrace our creativity, and we can share perspectives with others in a way we cannot when we rush through life from one task to another.

Divination has historically been gifted by two main routes: oracles and omens. Oracles are human conduits reaching the source of their prophetic messages through means of altered states. Often this has meant herbs, chemicals, trances, and most importantly dreams. Omens are messages observed by humans from a non-human source. Let us look at omens first.

The initial, almost scientific, ancient study of omens could be referred to as fledgling symbology at its very core. I wonder how Dan Brown would feel if he knew we were comparing his beloved Robert Langdon to an ancient Roman student of the entrails of sacrificial animals (see: *haruspex*).

Modern witches and witchmongers need not invoke the wrath of PETA to make use of the gifts omens can lend us. We have our choice of many beautiful tarot and other card decks, we have the 17th century practice of reading tea leaves, the ancient practice of reading the movement of the stars, and most importantly (and least capitalistically) reading the symbols around us.

Portents occur around us every day -- we see repeating numbers on a digital clock face, we see a stray dog in the same spot two or three days in a row, we count odd numbers of crows picking through our trash, we see something out of place that strikes us awake as we go about our daily chores. These are all symbols to take mind of. We are so programmed to be busy that we bulldoze over these contemporary real life omens and are never given the time or space to reflect on them.

As for oracles I'll bet each individual reading this has received some kind of message from another plane during an altered state: by way of dreams! Dream incubation, having a sleep ritual, teas of herbs to support your psychic meanderings, meditation, chanting, using specific music to reach a trance-like state, cannabis and mushrooms have all been used by cultures across the globe to reach a plane of consciousness and glean tidbits about their internal or external world. (Again, I hold no judgement on the usage of herbs and natural compounds but do encourage each practitioner to be mindful of the legality of these substances in the countries and regions where they are currently practicing.)

That is a large part of what this book is about. It's about taking heed of the omens in daily life, of the dreams in your unconscious mind, and in the other related practices we cultivate. We will explore the history of these traditions and hopefully reach a point where we can collectively realize that there is only benefit from being a little more observant, introspective, self-cultivating, and open-minded.

History

The Snake as Cultural Commonality

IF THE SNAKE IS REPRESENTATIVE OF mysteries, the chthonic, and the occult, then snake witchery is all about divination, empowerment, the human subconscious, and amassing knowledge. From Akkadian/Sumerian *barû* (seers practicing hydromancy and studying dreams) in 3000 BCE to the better-known Hellenic *pythia* or pythonesses (oracles translating the intent of gods while in a trance state) of 1400 BCE - 400 CE, the practitioners of mantic traditions throughout the Mediterranean, Asia, Africa, and Mesoamerica were allocated significant power and prestige.

Egyptian, Babylonian, Indian, Native American, Celtic, Nordic, Christian/Judaic, Ancient Cretan, Greco-Roman and many more cultures have shared in the archetype of the snake as emissary of the underworld, crawling out from the depths to deliver power, secret messages, spells, healing medicines, sacred knowledge, and more. Hereafter we discuss not only snakes, but also the related chthonic themes and deities, the underworld, mantic traditions, and connections cross-culturally.

In *The Greek Magical Papyri*, (a document exemplifying the spread of the mantic traditions of ancient Egypt into Mediterranean culture,) there is an incantation invoking the Egyptian goddess Sakhmet, which refers to the goddess as one "who has swallowed serpents" in which a request for a dream oracle be bestowed upon the invoker.[1]

The Egyptian goddess Weret Hekau, the "Great one of magic, great enchantress" was often depicted as a snake and protected against the dangers of the underworld, as the personification of supernatural powers. It is commonly believed that Weret Hekau or even Heqet (goddess of spring rites, fertility, and Nile flooding) were the origins of Hekate, the Greek goddess of magic and witchcraft, well-known to Neo-pagans.

Heqet was the mother of Heka (the deification of magic, closely entwined with Hu, the spoken utterance or command, i.e., a spell), and was consort of Khnum, the ram-headed guard of chthonic waters, subterranean guide and protector of the underworld.

Khnum himself overlapped a great deal with the official, widely-worshipped Egyption "god of the dead" and resurrection, Osiris. Being associated with flooding in Egypt in this period, as both Khnum, Osiris, and Heqet were, was a very high honor. The resurrection associated with the annual procession of the seasons was a very serious matter to those living in the desert. These gods were literally gods of life *and* death.

There is an obvious evolution throughout all mythology and a tendency to overlap and morph throughout time as borders change and trade expands. As a result, the many shared facets of the chthonic gods in the Near East (and eventually the Homeric West) are very poignant in their shared domains. For instance, the words for 'ram' and 'soul' ("Ba") sound the same in Egyptian -- therefore "ram deities were at times regarded as appearances of other gods".[2] Banebdjedet was a goat-headed god in Egypt near Mendes, described as being

---

[1] TAUNTON, GWENDOLYN, *The Path of Shadows: Chthonic Gods, Oneiromancy, & Necromancy in Ancient Greece*, (Manticore Press, 2018), 119
[2] PINCH, GERALDINE, *Handbook of Egyptian Mythology*, 114-115

specifically the Ba of Osiris for example. It's an easy connection to make that this could be in part the reason why auspices were taken from the state of the entrails of sheep, lambs, rams, and goats (haruscopy and even hepatoscopy), if these animals were culturally associated with the divine matter of the gods themselves.

These Egyptian examples are the first recorded occurrences of horned ruminants being associated with the underworld, but not the last: continental Europe during the Middle Ages continued to build upon the notion that the devil, while diametrically opposed to the notion of life-giving underworld gods, was apt to take the form of either a man with a goat's head or a bipedal, anthropomorphized goat. These devils could supernaturally fly, walk around the woods at night, chancing upon innocent townsfolk and coercing them to sign their souls away in his book in exchange for power. Baphomet in contemporary art and literature continues to serve this same purpose with a little more flair.

The Caduceus, the entwined serpents in a double helix, (sometimes incorporating a staff, sometimes wings, but not originally) were symbols of ophiolatry across Asia before gracing Hellenic Greece. In India in the third century BCE, the Caduceus was featured as Buddhist King Ashokha's personal mudra on punch coins from the third century BCE. In Sumeria both on ancient cuneiform scrolls[3] and on vases, drinking vessels and other relics, the god of vegetation and the underworld, Ningishzida ("Lord of the good tree") was symbolized by the Caduceus as early as 2100 BCE. Ningishzida was often depicted as having snakes flowing from his shoulders, or even occasionally took the form of a great snake with a man's head. The symbol of the intertwined snakes was co-opted by the fleet messenger god of communication, Hermes and a rudimentary single snake wrapped around a staff was the symbol of the healing god-son of Apollo, Asklepios. Long after a snake crawled across the ground to deliver healing herbs to Asklepios, the symbol of the Caduceus is still

---

[3] KOSAMBI, DAMODAR DHARMANAND, *Indian Numismatics*, (Orient Longman, 1981), 73

used to signify medicine, hospitals, and doctors.

Egyptian gods Ptah and Thoth, Greek god Hermes, and other "architect gods" are associated with occult snake wisdom -- from the Caduceus to their threefold forms, their domains of wisdom and transitional between-spaces all point to ancient man relating creation and enlightenment with the snake and the underworld.[4]

There is a class of powerful beings in Hinduism, Buddhism, and Jainism called *Naga* ("serpent"), which are half human and half snake or cobra. Beautiful and strong, they dwell in the underworld among ostentation, riches, and their intricate and architecturally-advanced palaces. Naga could be either dangerous or beneficial to humans, much like any other serpent or chthonic god. A Naga protected the Buddha from harsh rain for seven days while the Buddha meditated. There is a strong association with the archetypically psychic or dreamlike waters as well. Duality is exemplified in the tales of two prominent nagas, Shesha and Vasuki, who were associated with the Hindu creation myths and the churning of the cosmic ocean of milk.[5]

In many Slavic and Nordic cultures the snake is viewed as having a strong earth and time connection. In 1955 the Snake Witch (*Ormhäxan*) stone was discovered in Sweden depicting a snake-waving woman from around 400-600 AD in either Celtic or Norse styling, weaving what appears to be a spell. Nose mythical figure, Jormungandr, the World Serpent, was the bridge between planes, connecting the ethereal heavens with the chthonic. He was associated with both the creation and the destruction of the world cycle (similar to the abstract Egyptian chaos snake god, Apophis). The Greeks incubated dreams with particular attention paid to time and especially the sacred place of the dreamer, often arranging special omen-seeking pilgrimages.

Indigenous North American tribes believed the snake to represent wisdom, and use shed snakeskin and totems as sources of power. Horned Serpents within Eastern Tribes were widespread and very similar to the function of the Indian Naga, originating from the

---

[4] GARDINER, PHILIP, *Secret Societies*, (New Page Books, 2007), 122
[5] *Encyclopedia Britannica*, [Online Available], http://www.britannica.com

depths (this time hailing from under the water) and being perhaps dangerous but also benevolent. To the West, the Hopi Snake Dance remains one of the tribe's most important ceremonial dances.

Depicted as the Vision Snake, the "Feathered Serpents", *Kukulkan* (Mayan) and *Quetzalcoatl* (Aztec) were important Mesoamerican gods. Snakes themselves were regarded as the portals between two worlds in these cultures. Quetzalcoatl was associated with the creation of mankind as well as with the morning star (Venus).

This is a connection with the Biblical Lucifer, likely both associated with the morning star, Venus due to the planet's idiosyncratic procession. As Venus is not always visible in the night sky an onlooker might either decipher these movements as the serpentine portals between worlds appearing and disappearing, or as witnessing an angel fall from the sky to earth or into the underworld. Prior to becoming a Biblical villain, Lucifer or "light bringer" was the personification of the dawn, a Roman god. So mundane was this usage that Roman poet Catullus coined the moniker "Noctifer" to ascribe Venus her dusk characteristics:

> *Cernitis, innūptae, iuvenēs? cōnsurgite contrā;*
> *nīmīrum Oetaeōs ostendit Noctifer ignēs.*

> *See ye, maidens, the youths? Rise up to meet them.*
> *For sure the night-star shows his Oetaean fires.*

The list goes on: The Morrigan, Celtic Phantom Queen and forteller of doom and death in battle is not only associated with fate, but with the triple snake and as a triple goddess. The Morrigan was the liminal goddess, as she was the one that ushered the souls of the dead between realms.

Hekate, Greek goddess of magic, witchcraft, the underworld, crossroads, herbs and more was another triple goddess assigned to the liminal, transitional spaces where realms met. She was a titan born of Asteria ('the starry one') and Perses ('the Destroyer').[6] She had a strong following among the witches at Thessaly as well as in Asia Minor. With black doom-foretelling dogs, "crowned with oak leaves and the coils of wild serpents", Hekate was a common namesake for children, not a trait of gods deemed undesirable.[7] Keeper of keys and bearer of torches, she is often portrayed in her triple form as associated with Persephone (goddess of spring, vegetation, and the underworld) and Diana (goddess of the moon).

Before the Hellenic period, in Minoan Crete there was worshipped an otherwise-unnamed goddess, the Mistress (*Despoena*). Ancient sculptures similar to the Ormhaxan, of a bare-breasted woman waving an undulating snake in each hand, were uncovered near sites with chthonic labyrinth connotations. Later the Mistress was strongly associated with Persephone and the powerful triple goddess, as well as the Eleusinian Mysteries.

The Hebrew word for snake is נָחָשׁ (*nachash*), which is the same word for sorcery or witchcraft. The verb לְנַחֵשׁ (*Le-nachesh*) means 'to make a witchcraft' in the Hebrew Bible. In 220 CE Hippolytus wrote about what he called the Ophites and Naassenes (Christian sects) who honor snakes and prefer snakes to the idea of the tangible ideal of Christ. These sects indicate he was a parable for sacred power, and even go on to say that Eve in the Biblical garden of Eden believed the serpent to be the actual son of God. Epiphanius relates a similar tale, but describes the Ophites as not preferring snakes to Christ, but that the Ophites saw snakes and Christ as identical -- that the serpent of Eden blessed the human fore-parents with knowledge of good and evil instead of viewing it as a curse. There is yet another sect written about later that seems similar in most respects, the Nicolaitans, who are also mentioned in *Revelations*.

Interestingly, Irenaeus describes some of the Christian Ophite "heresies", including the development during creation of a beautiful Holy Spirit, the first woman and mother of the Incorruptible Light

---

[6] D'ESTES, SORITA & RANKINE, DAVID, *Hekate: Liminal Rites*, (Avalonia, 2009), 25
[7] SOPHOCLES, *The Root-Cutters*, 5 BCE

(Christ). The Holy Spirit gives birth again, this time to a woman who fell to earth: Sophia, or Wisdom. The most interesting might be several steps later in the Ophite creation myth, a 'false god', *Ialdabaoth*, the demiurge (another word for an architect god) (parallel to the traditional Christian god we know), creates many abstract sons (six, and then he rests). Last among these sons is *Ophiomorphus*, the snake embodying intellect, thought, and philosophy. It's riveting to think that even a short 200 years after the Christian Messiah's alleged death that there were multiple sects of Christianity that ascribed to a more Promethean view of the serpent of Eden (and a less misogynist worldview).

As you can tell, cultures throughout history see no problem in relating the mantic and sophic concepts. Only recently in our history have we divorced the subconscious and the feeling from science and knowledge. The tradition of the snake begs to differ.

2021 Exploration & Goals

Personal Mottos & Beliefs

What beliefs and personal mottos are my focus?

THE MOST IMPORTANT FOUNDATIONAL step in setting out for this year is knowing thyself. As it stands now, you're at the head of the year with twelve or more months ahead of you ripe for the picking: what beliefs do you feel are vital to the core of your being?

This should be a place for you to return to and reflect as often as is valuable to you -- review these tenets daily, weekly, or monthly. These adages will be here during the difficult times to remind you of who and what you are so you can recalibrate, heal, and pursue what truly matters. When you're in emergency mode it's easy to think that everything is worth saving because you don't have time to reflect before you dive in with your life preserver. Instead of feeling like you're constantly in emergency mode, putting out one fire after the next, this method will remind you that some fires you're presented with can be left to smolder while you take care of you.

I personally like to take some significant time to complete the next several sections and fully map out my year all in one night. This step has blossomed into a helpful ritual at the end of each year/beginning of the next. If you haven't the resource of time, they're broken down into shorter sections to move through one at a time.

So take a break, ensure you're calm and in a space where you will not be interrupted, and take five or ten minutes to determine what's most important to you. Light a candle, drink some tea and chill out.

Beliefs

Here are my 10 most important beliefs about life or myself:

★

★

★

★

★

★

★

★

★

★

Mottos, Adages, & A Pact

Here are the top 3 mottos I will use as a guide to navigate my life this year:

★

★

★

What are three things you know will come up this year that you recognize are things that will derail you from your personal mission?:

★

★

★

What are you going to say to yourself or to the person requesting these unreasonable things to you? (As politely as you need to, of course!)

★

★

★

If you can successfully establish these boundaries when the items above pop up to derail you, what will you say to yourself in gratitude?:

If you can successfully establish these boundaries when the items above pop up to derail you, what will you do for yourself in gratitude?:

Sign below to acknowledge this Pact you have made with yourself: I do so vow to treat myself how I would like to be treated and to take the types of actions I have outlined above:

_____

That's a lot of hard work. Take a second to consider how you feel about it. Do you feel optimistic? Perhaps a bit nervous? Write down your observations to review at the end of the year:

Now consider sharing your goals and motivations with a close friend. You'll help to hold yourself accountable and you may also inspire the people you care about to make these positive changes for themselves.

Visions & Goals:

Let's start thinking about how your future will look once you stick to the Pact. Where do you see yourself in 1 year, 3 years, 5 years, and 10 years? What would you like to achieve?:

In one year:

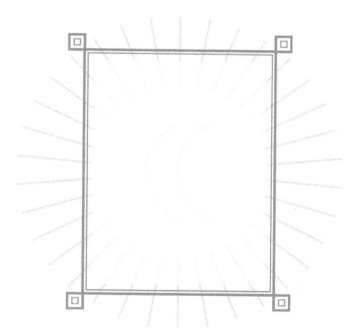

In three years:

In five years:

In ten years:

Hidden Signs

Omens from your Tarot Deck

NOW TO BEGIN YOUR DIVINATION. This will be your first omen reading for the coming year. Most New Agers and witches will either have experience with or exposure to tarot or other oracle cards and tiles. You may begin your year with either a three- or twelve-card spread (or both).

You'll need your own deck. I know many individuals with multiple decks of a kind and also as many opinions on how to appropriate and consecrate your decks -- how to read reversals, if your first deck need be gifted, etc. I hold none of these superstitions with particularly high regard, but do assert that you should stick with whatever belief you personally hold or tradition you were handed down. Some decks' creators will pass along information on whether your reversals should be read with an alternate meaning or not, but I have observed that in working with each individual deck you'll notice it tell you how to be interpreted over time. As in all things it will be most valuable to listen to your intuition as you hone your craft.

As in all occult practices it's important to come to the space in which you're divining with intent and set aside time to be uninterrupted or else risk an occluded meaning. I personally like to do this reading for the year to come on the darkest day of the preceding year, but choose a time that feels right to you.

As far as a three- or twelve-card spread, let me outline some differences: The three-card spread is flexible and direct. Most prominent use throughout the decades has been the Past/Present/Future layout. This easily works in a reading aimed at the coming year. For the purposes of self-discovery another of my preferred readings might be one's own Material/Emotional/Spiritual states or the very pertinent Self/Current Path/Potential.

The twelve-card spread is what I use each year for mine and my friends' readings. The reading is essentially one card per month and often I'll draw one thirteenth card as a Theme or Lesson omen. This has proven useful to provide overarching context and a definitive time period to apply each message to.

For each reading type be sure to record your intentions in the spread (especially for the flexible three-card spread) and interpretations for reflection throughout the year.

Three-Card Spread

Date:
Intentions:

Cards:

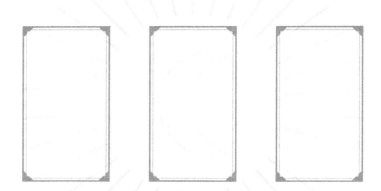

Interpretation:

Twelve-Card Spread

Date:

Intentions:

Cards:

Interpretation:

Mel Despoenae Labyrinthī

"TO THE MISTRESS OF THE LABYRINTH: honey." While the title above is in latin, its equivalent was found in a syllabic script[8] on a tablet in ancient Crete at Knossos, referring to the offerings made to "all the gods" and also to the Great Goddess of the winding, dancing maze of earth we know as a labyrinth. (Fun fact: the offerings made there were *equal* -- one jar of honey to split amongst all the gods, and one jar of honey proffered to the Mistress herself.)

We discussed symbols such as the labyrinth indicative of secret knowledge and the various figures attributed as keepers in the History chapter of this book, but now we will focus on the sweetness in life -- or the joy to be found in the coming year: the honey if you will. These will be the cheer and amusements you wish to pepper throughout the coming months in embrace of life's simple pleasures.

There is a space to record your To Be Read list of books, your book club list if you belong to (or wish to form) such a coalition, as well as a Mileage page for tracking how far you've come in any sense

---

[8] Called Linear B, this script predating the Greek alphabet was used in Mycenaean Greek writing as early as 1450 B.C.E.

of the word you'd like to ascribe.

Projects

Title: Due:

Steps:

Title: Due:

Steps:

Title: Due:

Steps:

Title: *Due:*

Steps:

Title: *Due:*

Steps:

Title: *Due:*

Steps:

Title: *Due:*

Steps:

Title: *Due:*

Steps:

Title: *Due:*

Steps:

2021 To Be Read List

- ★
- ★
- ★
- ★
- ★
- ★
- ★
- ★
- ★
- ★
- ★
- ★
- ★
- ★
- ★
- ★
- ★
- ★
- ★
- ★
- ★
- ★
- ★
- ★
- ★
- ★
- ★
- ★

2021 Top TBR By Genre

★ Comic/Graphic Novel:

★ Banned Book:

★ Sci-Fi:

★ Posthumously Published:

★ Recommended by a Friend:

★ Book-to-Movie 2021:

★ Thriller/Suspense:

★ Started, Never Finished:

★ Based on a True Story:

★ Beautiful Cover:

★ Translated to English:

★ Award-winner:

★ Self-Improvement:

★ Recommended by an Indie Bookseller:

★ Favorite Author's Favorite Author:

★ Female Lead:

★ Feminist theory/Essay/Agenda:

★ Written by Dual Authors:

★ Title Mentioned in Another Book You've Read:

★ Set in New England:

2021 Book Club

1. *Title:*   *Due Date:*
   Author: *Rating:*
2. *Title:*   *Due Date:*
   Author: *Rating:*
3. *Title:*   *Due Date:*
   Author: *Rating:*
4. *Title:*   *Due Date:*
   Author: *Rating:*
5. *Title:*   *Due Date:*
   Author: *Rating:*
6. *Title:*   *Due Date:*
   Author: *Rating:*
7. *Title:*   *Due Date:*
   Author: *Rating:*
8. *Title:*   *Due Date:*
   Author: *Rating:*
9. *Title:*   *Due Date:*
   Author: *Rating:*
10. *Title:*   *Due Date:*
    Author: *Rating:*
11. *Title:*   *Due Date:*
    Author: *Rating:*
12. *Title:*   *Due Date:*
    Author: *Rating:*

2021 Monthly Mileage

Run, read, walk, swim, drive -- no matter what you measure, list your days/pages/miles/mountains/woods traveled down here to see how far you've come in one year's time:

★ *January:*

★ *February:*

★ *March:*

★ *April:*

★ *May:*

★ *June:*

★ *July:*

★ *August:*

★ *September:*

★ *October:*

★ *November:*

★ *December:*

Gregorian Calendar & Lunations

THE CALENDAR WE EMPLOY TODAY is called the Gregorian calendar. Though named after and implemented by Catholic Pope Gregory XIII in 1582 C.E., witches and witchmongers of various other denominations, religions, and those existing from without the bounds of the sacred need not fear or begrudge the usage: though generally considered Catholic, the initial problem this calendar aimed to solve in 1582 was that of the holy day of Easter lapsing too far from the spring equinox -- a rather solar and perhaps pagan problem for the namesake of Pope Gregory I to have.[9]

The Gregorian calendar was not even developed by the Pope but by an Italian doctor, astronomer, and philosopher Aloysius Lilius -- so a more appropriate name would be the Lilian calendar.

As follows will be a monthly layout for 15 months (2021 plus a preceding 3 months), a weekly layout, and pages for your particular rituals during the lunations of each new and full moon. Following the close of each month there is a reflection section to journal and

---

[9] Pope Gregory I was the first pope to launch a mission from Rome in hopes to convert the pagan Anglo-Saxons from England.

observe the meaning through your mantic practices.

In hec [occultīs] signis vinces.

In these hidden signs shall you conquer.

2020

October - December

October

A Halloween Full Moon

THE PLACEMENT OF THE MOON IN TAURUS signifies a comfortable, aesthetic end to the harvest season -- and the moon revels in its placement. Perfect for an 'eat, drink, and be merry' holiday vibe, this happenstance is a rare one as well: The next Halloween full moon won't occur for another 19 years, in 2039. This pattern is known as the Metonic cycle.

It's not all fun and games (with many planets/asteroids retrograde and the quincunx aspect still being dominant), we're still under the spell of 2020's looming "rock and a hard place" energy; but Scorpio season and planets Venus and Neptune in exaltation do their best to compliment the Moon to let your senses lead you off into a dreamy, festive evening.

October

DO NOT FORGET	MONDAY	TUESDAY	WEDNESDAY
	5	6	7
	12	13	14
	19	20	21
	26	27	28

Notes

OMENS   BOOKS   SONGS

THURSDAY	FRIDAY	SATURDAY	SUNDAY
♈ 1	2	3	4
8	9	10	11
15 ♎	16	17	18
22	23	24	25
29	30 ♉	31	

Works

| PROJECTS | NEW MOON | FULL MOON |

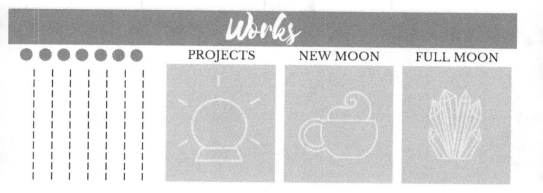

DATES:

Weekly

PERSONAL LIST

WORK LIST

Focuses

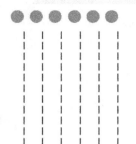

MY SPIRIT

MY LOVED ONES

MY WORKS

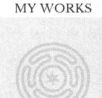

MONDAY

TUESDAY

WEDNESDAY

THURSDAY

FRIDAY

SATURDAY

SUNDAY

Weekly Notes

DREAMS

WHY?

MONEY

TOTAL

DATES:

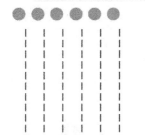

Weekly

PERSONAL LIST

WORK LIST

Focuses

MY SPIRIT   MY LOVED ONES   MY WORKS

MONDAY

TUESDAY

WEDNESDAY

THURSDAY

FRIDAY

SATURDAY

SUNDAY

Weekly Notes

DREAMS	WHY?	MONEY

TOTAL

DATES:

Weekly

PERSONAL LIST

WORK LIST

Focuses

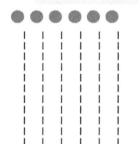 MY SPIRIT  MY LOVED ONES  MY WORKS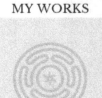

MONDAY

TUESDAY

WEDNESDAY

THURSDAY

FRIDAY

SATURDAY

SUNDAY

Weekly Notes

DREAMS

WHY?

MONEY

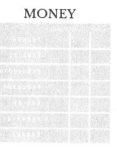

TOTAL

DATES: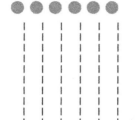

Weekly

PERSONAL LIST

WORK LIST

Focuses

MY SPIRIT   MY LOVED ONES   MY WORKS

MONDAY

TUESDAY

WEDNESDAY

THURSDAY

FRIDAY

SATURDAY

SUNDAY

Weekly Notes

DREAMS

WHY?

MONEY

TOTAL

DATES:

Weekly

PERSONAL LIST

WORK LIST

Focuses

MY SPIRIT

MY LOVED ONES

MY WORKS

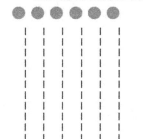

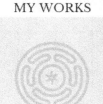

MONDAY

TUESDAY

WEDNESDAY

THURSDAY

FRIDAY

SATURDAY

SUNDAY

Weekly Notes

DREAMS

WHY?

MONEY

TOTAL

DATE:

NEW MOON INTENTION:

I EVALUATE & FEEL:

INTENTION TO BREAK OR CREATE:

I GIVE:

New Moon: To Bestow

INTENTION I

INTENTION II

INTENTION III

I INITIATE/I HATCH:

Full Moon:
To Expel

NEW MOON INTENTION:

I EVALUATE & FEEL:

INTENTION TO BREAK OR CREATE:

I GIVE:

Dream Reflections

What am I trying to tell myself?

Trends:

Pieces I'm Struck By:

People Involved:

Emotions Experienced:

Archetypes Identified:

Repeated Symbols:

Traditional Meanings:

Personal Meanings Divined Thus Far:

(use the next page to sketch necessary elements)

Tarot Reflections

What am I being told?

Interpretations:

Reflections on Loved Ones

What do I want to remember?

★
★
★
★
★
★
★
★
★
★
★
★
★
★
★
★
★
★
★

Inner Reflections

What do I think?

What are 3 things that went well?

What were 3 low points?

What did I learn?

Things I'd like to repeat?

Things I want to do differently?

What would I use a wish to change?

When did I feel most alive?

What relationships do I want to improve?

What did I waste time on?

Reflections on Books

What did I read?

_____
_____
_____
_____
_____
_____
_____
_____
_____
_____
_____
_____
_____
_____
_____
_____
_____
_____

Gratitude

What am I thankful for?

_____

_____

_____

_____

_____

_____

_____

_____

_____

_____

_____

_____

_____

_____

_____

_____

_____

_____

November

A Mourning Blood Moon & the Liberator

THE PLACEMENT OF THE MOON IN GEMINI signifies a frenetic transition from fall into winter and the very end of the year. A Mourning Moon is the final Full Moon prior to the Winter Solstice -- and so fitting for 2020. The moon is amplified in its wild, changing emotions by the presence of Uranus rising. The Liberator planet brings its own inconsistencies so just be mindful during this liminal time not to push others away despite holiday stress.

Despite these hallmarks of chaos, a stellium of planets lingering in responsible, grave Capricorn serve to anchor us, and Mars remains in exaltation in Aries and left retrograde just a few short weeks prior.

November

DO NOT FORGET	MONDAY	TUESDAY	WEDNESDAY
		2	3	4
	9	10	11
	16	17	18
	23	24	25
	30 ♊		

Notes

● ● ● ● ● ●

OMENS	BOOKS	SONGS

full moon: 11/30 ♊

THURSDAY	FRIDAY	SATURDAY	SUNDAY
			1
5	6	7	8
12	13	14 ♏	15
19	20	21	22
26	27	28	29

Works

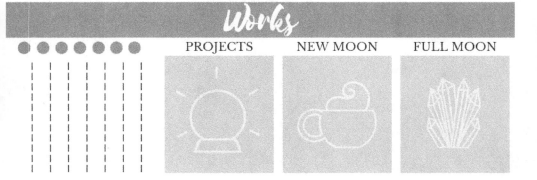

PROJECTS   NEW MOON   FULL MOON

Weekly

PERSONAL LIST

WORK LIST

Focuses

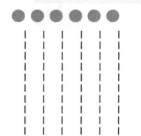

MY SPIRIT

MY LOVED ONES

MY WORKS

MONDAY

TUESDAY

WEDNESDAY

THURSDAY

FRIDAY

SATURDAY

SUNDAY

Weekly Notes

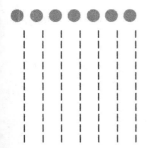

DREAMS

WHY?

MONEY

TOTAL

DATES:

Weekly

PERSONAL LIST

WORK LIST

Focuses

MY SPIRIT

MY LOVED ONES

MY WORKS

MONDAY

TUESDAY

WEDNESDAY

THURSDAY

FRIDAY

SATURDAY

SUNDAY

Weekly Notes

DREAMS

WHY?

MONEY

TOTAL

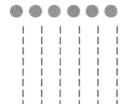

Weekly

PERSONAL LIST

WORK LIST

Focuses

MY SPIRIT   MY LOVED ONES   MY WORKS

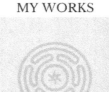

MONDAY

TUESDAY

WEDNESDAY

THURSDAY

FRIDAY

SATURDAY

SUNDAY

Weekly Notes

DREAMS

WHY?

MONEY

TOTAL

DATES:

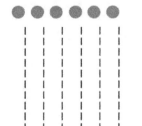

Weekly

PERSONAL LIST	WORK LIST

Focuses

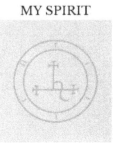

MY SPIRIT   MY LOVED ONES   MY WORKS

MONDAY

TUESDAY

WEDNESDAY

THURSDAY

FRIDAY

SATURDAY

SUNDAY

Weekly Notes

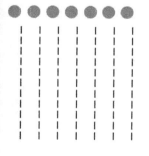

DREAMS

WHY?

MONEY

TOTAL

New Moon: To Bestow

INTENTION I

INTENTION II

INTENTION III

I INITIATE/I HATCH:

NEW MOON INTENTION:

I EVALUATE & FEEL:

INTENTION TO BREAK OR CREATE:

I GIVE:

Tarot Reflections

What am I being told?

Interpretations:

Reflections on Loved Ones

What do I want to remember?

★
★
★
★
★
★
★
★
★
★
★
★
★
★
★
★
★
★
★

Inner Reflections

What do I think?

What are 3 things that went well?

What were 3 low points?

What did I learn?

Things I'd like to repeat?

Things I want to do differently?

What would I use a wish to change?

When did I feel most alive?

What relationships do I want to improve?

What did I waste time on?

Reflections on Books

What did I read?

_____
_____
_____
_____
_____
_____
_____
_____
_____
_____
_____
_____
_____
_____
_____
_____
_____
_____
_____
_____

Gratitude

What am I thankful for?

_____
_____
_____
_____
_____
_____
_____
_____
_____
_____
_____
_____
_____
_____
_____
_____
_____
_____
_____

December

A Cold Moon Crescendo

THE PLACEMENT OF THE MOON IN CANCER signifies an emotional boon with silver disc in the sign of its exaltation despite a few challenging aspects at the end of a challenging year: The North Node is rising, heralding perhaps issues with either finding or connecting with the self while 9 square aspects simultaneously create tension and bring a few obstacles our way. This is all magnified of course by Jupiter, the King planet and bringer of expansion and luck (good or bad) .

It's been a crazy year -- be sure to take time to check in with yourself and take it easy.

December

DO NOT FORGET	MONDAY	TUESDAY	WEDNESDAY
		1	2
	7	8	9
♐	14	15	16
	21	22	23
	28 ♋	29	30

Notes

● ● ● ● ● ●

OMENS	BOOKS	SONGS

THURSDAY	FRIDAY	SATURDAY	SUNDAY
3	4	5	6
10	11	12	13
17	18	19	20
24	25	26	27
31			

Works

PROJECTS   NEW MOON   FULL MOON

DATES:

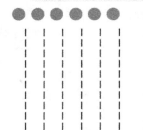

Weekly

PERSONAL LIST

WORK LIST

Focuses

MY SPIRIT | MY LOVED ONES | MY WORKS

MONDAY

TUESDAY

WEDNESDAY

THURSDAY

FRIDAY

SATURDAY

SUNDAY

Weekly Notes

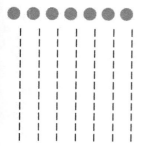

DREAMS

WHY?

MONEY

TOTAL

DATES:

Weekly

PERSONAL LIST

WORK LIST

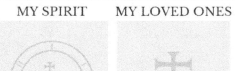

Focuses

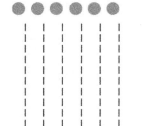

MY SPIRIT

MY LOVED ONES

MY WORKS

MONDAY

TUESDAY

WEDNESDAY

THURSDAY

FRIDAY

SATURDAY

SUNDAY

Weekly Notes

DREAMS	WHY?	MONEY

TOTAL

DATES:

Weekly

PERSONAL LIST

WORK LIST

Focuses

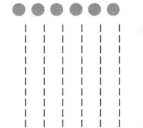

MY SPIRIT

MY LOVED ONES

MY WORKS

MONDAY

TUESDAY

WEDNESDAY

THURSDAY

FRIDAY

SATURDAY

SUNDAY

Weekly Notes

| DREAMS | WHY? | MONEY |

TOTAL

DATES: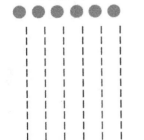

Weekly

PERSONAL LIST

WORK LIST

Focuses

 MY SPIRIT

MY LOVED ONES

MY WORKS

MONDAY

TUESDAY

WEDNESDAY

THURSDAY

FRIDAY

SATURDAY

SUNDAY

Weekly Notes

DREAMS

WHY?

MONEY

TOTAL

DATES:

Weekly

PERSONAL LIST

WORK LIST

Focuses

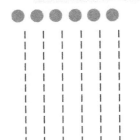

MY SPIRIT   MY LOVED ONES   MY WORKS

MONDAY

TUESDAY

WEDNESDAY

THURSDAY

FRIDAY

SATURDAY

SUNDAY

Weekly Notes

DREAMS

WHY?

MONEY

TOTAL

INTENTION I

INTENTION II

INTENTION III

I INITIATE/I HATCH:

NEW MOON INTENTION:

I EVALUATE & FEEL:

INTENTION TO BREAK OR CREATE:

I GIVE:

Dream Reflections

What am I trying to tell myself?

Trends:

Pieces I'm Struck By:

People Involved:

Emotions Experienced:

Archetypes Identified:

Repeated Symbols:

Traditional Meanings:

Personal Meanings Divined Thus Far:

(use the next page to sketch necessary elements)

Tarot Reflections

What am I being told?

Interpretations:

Reflections on Loved Ones

What do I want to remember?

★
★
★
★
★
★
★
★
★
★
★
★
★
★
★
★
★
★
★

Inner Reflections

What do I think?

What are 3 things that went well?

What were 3 low points?

What did I learn?

Things I'd like to repeat?

Things I want to do differently?

What would I use a wish to change?

When did I feel most alive?

What relationships do I want to improve?

What did I waste time on?

Reflections on Books

What did I read?

Gratitude

What am I thankful for?

2021

January - December

January

A Sensitive Cold Moon

THE PLACEMENT OF THE MOON IN LEO signifies strongly-felt emotions prone to outbursts -- whether they be outbursts of glee or tantrums is dependent upon the astral environment, and this stage is not going to be an easy one for the Lion. Neptune, bestower of dreams and spiritual gifts, graces the Nadir and nudges the Moon into an extra sensitive mood. Beware of what you may be stubborn about at this time, as a Grand Fire Trine can make these leonine outbursts particularly brash.

With it being Aquarius season *and* the Moon Square Aquarian ruler Uranus, you may also feel a bit more scrutinized or alone in your emotions. It might be a constructive time to use those Leo/Neptune creative gifts a bit more introspectively.

January

DO NOT FORGET	MONDAY	TUESDAY	WEDNESDAY
	4	5	6
	11	12 ≈	13
	18	19	20
	25	26	27

Notes

● ● ● ● ● ●

OMENS	BOOKS	SONGS

THURSDAY	FRIDAY	SATURDAY	SUNDAY
	1	2	3
7	8	9	10
14	15	16	17
21	22	23	24
♌ 28	29	30	31

Works

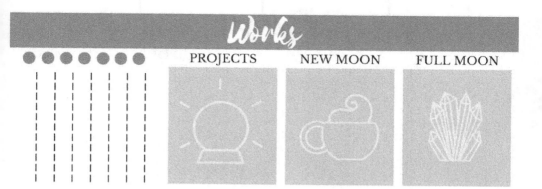

PROJECTS   NEW MOON   FULL MOON

DATES:

Weekly

PERSONAL LIST

WORK LIST

Focuses

MY SPIRIT   MY LOVED ONES   MY WORKS

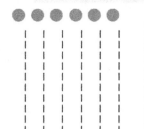 

MONDAY

TUESDAY

WEDNESDAY

THURSDAY

FRIDAY

SATURDAY

SUNDAY

Weekly Notes

DREAMS

WHY?

MONEY

TOTAL

DATES:

Weekly

PERSONAL LIST

WORK LIST

Focuses

MY SPIRIT   MY LOVED ONES   MY WORKS

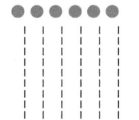

MONDAY

TUESDAY

WEDNESDAY

THURSDAY

FRIDAY

SATURDAY

SUNDAY

Weekly Notes

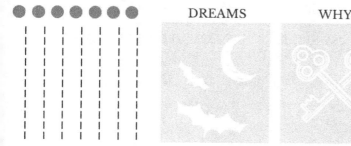

DREAMS

WHY?

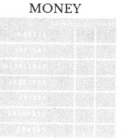

MONEY

TOTAL

DATES:

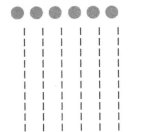

Weekly

PERSONAL LIST

WORK LIST

Focuses

 MY SPIRIT

 MY LOVED ONES

 MY WORKS

MONDAY

TUESDAY

WEDNESDAY

THURSDAY

FRIDAY

SATURDAY

SUNDAY

Weekly Notes

DREAMS	WHY?	MONEY

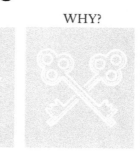

TOTAL

DATES:

Weekly

PERSONAL LIST

WORK LIST

Focuses

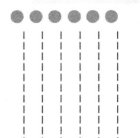

MY SPIRIT

MY LOVED ONES

MY WORKS

MONDAY

TUESDAY

WEDNESDAY

THURSDAY

FRIDAY

SATURDAY

SUNDAY

Weekly Notes

DREAMS

WHY?

MONEY

TOTAL

DATE:

New Moon:
To Bestow

INTENTION I

INTENTION II

INTENTION III

I INITIATE/I HATCH:

NEW MOON INTENTION:

I EVALUATE & FEEL:

INTENTION TO BREAK OR CREATE:

I GIVE:

Dream Reflections

What am I trying to tell myself?

Trends:

Pieces I'm Struck By:

People Involved:

Emotions Experienced:

Archetypes Identified:

Repeated Symbols:

Traditional Meanings:

Personal Meanings Divined Thus Far:

(use the next page to sketch necessary elements)

Tarot Reflections

What am I being told?

Interpretations:

Reflections on Loved Ones

What do I want to remember?

★
★
★
★
★
★
★
★
★
★
★
★
★
★
★
★
★
★
★

Inner Reflections

What do I think?

What are 3 things that went well?

What were 3 low points?

What did I learn?

Things I'd like to repeat?

Things I want to do differently?

What would I use a wish to change?

When did I feel most alive?

What relationships do I want to improve?

What did I waste time on?

Reflections on Books

What did I read?

_____
_____
_____
_____
_____
_____
_____
_____
_____
_____
_____
_____
_____
_____
_____
_____
_____
_____

February

A Focused Snow Moon

THE PLACEMENT OF THE MOON IN VIRGO signifies a pointed sharp focus on your surroundings and how they affect your emotions. With several inner planets in Aquarius and with Mercury, Jupiter, and Saturn all descending, you likely will feel remarkably unwilling to communicate with others at this time.

Most planets are congregated in the top right quadrant of the astral caelum and the four elements are evenly distributed amongst the inner planets bringing a healthy approach to selfishness at this time. Embrace the urge to rearrange your space, clean out your computer files, and withdraw for a relaxing Saturday evening in. Neptune in Pisces is the sole dispositor and will likely bring the inspiration you need if you only give yourself the space to dwell.

February

DO NOT FORGET	MONDAY	TUESDAY	WEDNESDAY
	1	2	3
	8	9	10
	15	16	17
	22	23	24

Notes

OMENS   BOOKS   SONGS

THURSDAY	FRIDAY	SATURDAY	SUNDAY
4	5	6	7
≋ 11	12	13	14
18	19	20	21
25	26 ♍	27	28

Works

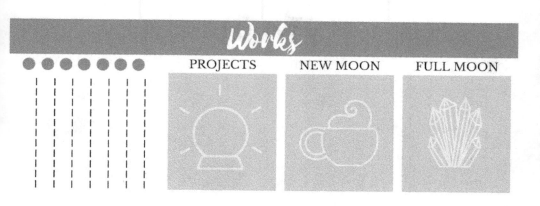

PROJECTS   NEW MOON   FULL MOON

DATES: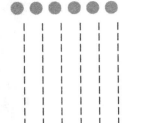

Weekly

PERSONAL LIST

WORK LIST

Focuses

● ● ● ● ● ●

MY SPIRIT

MY LOVED ONES

MY WORKS

MONDAY

TUESDAY

WEDNESDAY

THURSDAY

FRIDAY

SATURDAY

SUNDAY

Weekly Notes

DREAMS

WHY?

MONEY

TOTAL

DATES:

Weekly

PERSONAL LIST

WORK LIST

Focuses

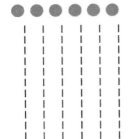

MY SPIRIT

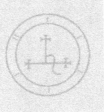

MY LOVED ONES

MY WORKS

MONDAY

TUESDAY

WEDNESDAY

THURSDAY

FRIDAY

SATURDAY

SUNDAY

Weekly Notes

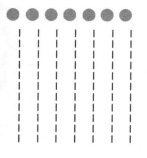

DREAMS

WHY?

MONEY

TOTAL

DATES: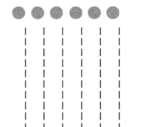

Weekly

PERSONAL LIST	WORK LIST

Focuses

MY SPIRIT	MY LOVED ONES	MY WORKS

MONDAY

TUESDAY

WEDNESDAY

THURSDAY

FRIDAY

SATURDAY

SUNDAY

Weekly Notes

DREAMS

WHY?

MONEY

TOTAL

DATES:

Weekly

PERSONAL LIST

WORK LIST

Focuses

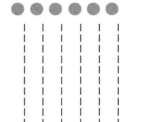

MY SPIRIT

MY LOVED ONES

MY WORKS

MONDAY

TUESDAY

WEDNESDAY

THURSDAY

FRIDAY

SATURDAY

SUNDAY

Weekly Notes

DREAMS

WHY?

MONEY

TOTAL

New Moon: To Bestow

INTENTION I

INTENTION II

INTENTION III

I INITIATE/I HATCH:

Full Moon: To Expel

NEW MOON INTENTION:

I EVALUATE & FEEL:

INTENTION TO BREAK OR CREATE:

I GIVE:

Dream Reflections

What am I trying to tell myself?

Trends:

Pieces I'm Struck By:

People Involved:

Emotions Experienced:

Archetypes Identified:

Repeated Symbols:

Traditional Meanings:

Personal Meanings Divined Thus Far:

(use the next page to sketch necessary elements)

Tarot Reflections

What am I being told?

Interpretations:

Reflections on Loved Ones

What do I want to remember?

★
★
★
★
★
★
★
★
★
★
★
★
★
★
★
★
★
★
★
★

Inner Reflections

What do I think?

What are 3 things that went well?

What were 3 low points?

What did I learn?

Things I'd like to repeat?

Things I want to do differently?

What would I use a wish to change?

When did I feel most alive?

What relationships do I want to improve?

What did I waste time on?

Reflections on Books

What did I read?

March

A Sap Moon Air Trine

THE PLACEMENT OF THE MOON IN LIBRA signifies an effortless elegance as the world awakens before spring. As the Sun and Venus join Chiron (the Wounded Healer) in fiery, childlike Aries, the balanced approach of a Libran Moon is just what the doctor ordered -- and as the sign in opposition to Aries is probably the only placement that could turn this season's "heal me, love me" attitude into something beautiful.

A Grand Air Trine involving this easygoing Moon breezes through the zeitgeist around Uranus, egging us to push above and beyond -- and you can bet this communicative Air trio will encourage us all to shout all our new thoughts from the mountaintops. Expect Spring Fevers to be amplified.

March

DO NOT FORGET	MONDAY	TUESDAY	WEDNESDAY
	1	2	3
	8	9	10
	15	16	17
	22	23	24
	29	30	31

Notes

OMENS   BOOKS   SONGS

THURSDAY	FRIDAY	SATURDAY	SUNDAY
4	5	6	7
11	12 ♓	13	14
18	19	20	21
25	26	27 ♎	28

Works

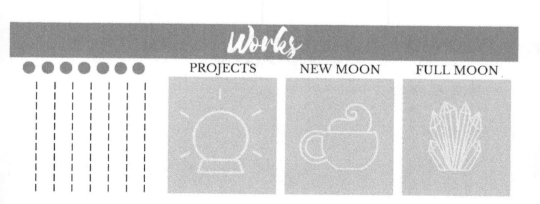

PROJECTS   NEW MOON   FULL MOON

DATES:

Weekly

PERSONAL LIST

WORK LIST

Focuses

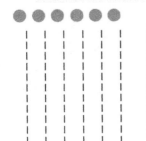

MY SPIRIT

MY LOVED ONES

MY WORKS

MONDAY

TUESDAY

WEDNESDAY

THURSDAY

FRIDAY

SATURDAY

SUNDAY

Weekly Notes

DREAMS

WHY?

MONEY

TOTAL

DATES:

Weekly

PERSONAL LIST

WORK LIST

Focuses

MY SPIRIT

MY LOVED ONES

MY WORKS

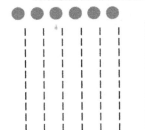

MONDAY

TUESDAY

WEDNESDAY

THURSDAY

FRIDAY

SATURDAY

SUNDAY

Weekly Notes

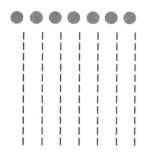

DREAMS

WHY?

MONEY

TOTAL

DATES:

Weekly

PERSONAL LIST

WORK LIST

Focuses

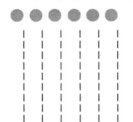

MY SPIRIT   MY LOVED ONES   MY WORKS

MONDAY

TUESDAY

WEDNESDAY

THURSDAY

FRIDAY

SATURDAY

SUNDAY

Weekly Notes

DREAMS	WHY?	MONEY

TOTAL

DATES:

Weekly

PERSONAL LIST

WORK LIST

Focuses

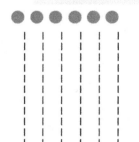

MY SPIRIT

MY LOVED ONES

MY WORKS

MONDAY

TUESDAY

WEDNESDAY

THURSDAY

FRIDAY

SATURDAY

SUNDAY

Weekly Notes

DREAMS

WHY?

MONEY

TOTAL

New Moon: To Bestow

INTENTION I

INTENTION II

INTENTION III

I INITIATE/I HATCH:

Full Moon: To Expel

DATE:

NEW MOON INTENTION:

I EVALUATE & FEEL:

INTENTION TO BREAK OR CREATE:

I GIVE:

Dream Reflections

What am I trying to tell myself?

Trends:

Pieces I'm Struck By:

People Involved:

Emotions Experienced:

Archetypes Identified:

Repeated Symbols:

Traditional Meanings:

Personal Meanings Divined Thus Far:

(use the next page to sketch necessary elements)

Tarot Reflections

What am I being told?

Interpretations:

Reflections on Loved Ones

What do I want to remember?

★
★
★
★
★
★
★
★
★
★
★
★
★
★
★
★
★
★
★

Inner Reflections

What do I think?

What are 3 things that went well?

What were 3 low points?

What did I learn?

Things I'd like to repeat?

Things I want to do differently?

What would I use a wish to change?

When did I feel most alive?

What relationships do I want to improve?

What did I waste time on?

Reflections on Books

What did I read?

Gratitude

What am I thankful for?

_____
_____
_____
_____
_____
_____
_____
_____
_____
_____
_____
_____
_____
_____
_____
_____
_____
_____

April

A Rich Hare Moon

THE PLACEMENT OF THE MOON IN SCORPIO signifies an intense, probing circumstance during this Supermoon. A stellium in fellow fixed sign, Taurus brings a very eldritch, chthonic earth goddess vibe. Neptune is descending and the heady, dreamy mist is fading fast, exposing this ancient and unyielding monolith that somehow always lurked beneath.

If this month were an island, a Grand Water Trine laps at the shores, lending profundity to the timeless fertility goddess and a warning to those who would defy her. While giving in to the luxury of self-indulgence is recommended at this time, beware the North Node conjunct the Midheaven, and unnecessary attention paid to your reputation and social trends.

April

DO NOT FORGET	MONDAY	TUESDAY	WEDNESDAY
	5	6	7
	12	13	14
	19	20	21
♏	26	27	28

supermoon

Notes

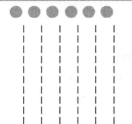

OMENS	BOOKS	SONGS

THURSDAY	FRIDAY	SATURDAY	SUNDAY
1	2	3	4
8	9	10 ♈	11
15	16	17	18
22	23	24	25
29	30		

Works

● ● ● ● ● ● ●

PROJECTS   NEW MOON   FULL MOON

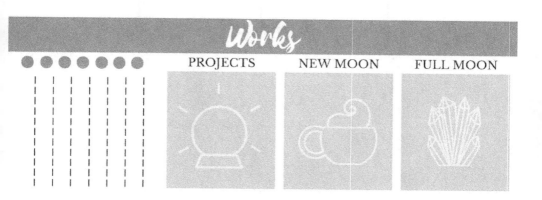

DATES:

Weekly

PERSONAL LIST

WORK LIST

Focuses

MY SPIRIT   MY LOVED ONES   MY WORKS

MONDAY

TUESDAY

WEDNESDAY

THURSDAY

FRIDAY

SATURDAY

SUNDAY

Weekly Notes

DREAMS

WHY?

MONEY

TOTAL

DATES:

Weekly

PERSONAL LIST

WORK LIST

Focuses

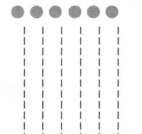

MY SPIRIT

MY LOVED ONES

MY WORKS

MONDAY

TUESDAY

WEDNESDAY

THURSDAY

FRIDAY

SATURDAY

SUNDAY

Weekly Notes

		DREAMS	WHY?	MONEY

TOTAL

DATES:

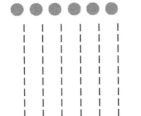

Weekly

PERSONAL LIST

WORK LIST

Focuses

MY SPIRIT

MY LOVED ONES

MY WORKS

MONDAY

TUESDAY

WEDNESDAY

THURSDAY

FRIDAY

SATURDAY

SUNDAY

Weekly Notes

DREAMS

WHY?

MONEY

TOTAL

DATES:

Weekly

PERSONAL LIST

WORK LIST

Focuses

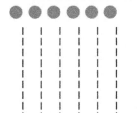

MY SPIRIT

MY LOVED ONES

MY WORKS

MONDAY

TUESDAY

WEDNESDAY

THURSDAY

FRIDAY

SATURDAY

SUNDAY

Weekly Notes

| | | | | | |

DREAMS

WHY?

MONEY

TOTAL

DATE:

INTENTION I

INTENTION II

INTENTION III

I INITIATE/I HATCH:

NEW MOON INTENTION:

I EVALUATE & FEEL:

INTENTION TO BREAK OR CREATE:

I GIVE:

Dream Reflections

What am I trying to tell myself?

Trends:

Pieces I'm Struck By:

People Involved:

Emotions Experienced:

Archetypes Identified:

Repeated Symbols:

Traditional Meanings:

Personal Meanings Divined Thus Far:

(use the next page to sketch necessary elements)

Tarot Reflections

What am I being told?

Interpretations:

Reflections on Loved Ones

What do I want to remember?

★
★
★
★
★
★
★
★
★
★
★
★
★
★
★
★
★
★
★

Inner Reflections

What do I think?

What are 3 things that went well?

What were 3 low points?

What did I learn?

Things I'd like to repeat?

Things I want to do differently?

What would I use a wish to change?

When did I feel most alive?

What relationships do I want to improve?

What did I waste time on?

Gratitude

What am I thankful for?

_____

_____

_____

_____

_____

_____

_____

_____

_____

_____

_____

_____

_____

_____

_____

_____

_____

_____

_____

May

A Wildflower Blood Supermoon

THE PLACEMENT OF THE MOON IN SAGITTARIUS signifies an unbridled enthusiasm with a desire for understanding of everyone's feelings -- amplified through the ultimate hype-man: a Supermoon Total Lunar eclipse (Blood Moon) *and* the twin Bose speakers of multiple Gemini placements. Chiron, the Wounded Healer is descending so we're finally alleviated from all of this exhausting self work and starting to turn our understanding outward.

With the Air element dominant among inner planets and Mercury in exaltation there should be a free flow of ideas, easy cooperation, and perhaps -- depending on your personal placements -- a road trip or unexpected woodland excursion.

May

| MONDAY | TUESDAY | WEDNESDAY

	3	4	5
	10 ♉	11	12
	17	18	19
	24	25 ♐	26
	31		*supermoon lunar eclipse*

Notes

OMENS   BOOKS   SONGS

THURSDAY	FRIDAY	SATURDAY	SUNDAY
		1	2
6	7	8	9
13	14	15	16
20	21	22	23
27	28	29	30

Works

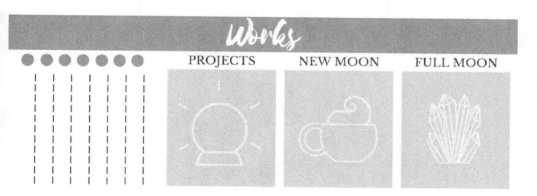

PROJECTS   NEW MOON   FULL MOON

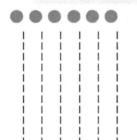
Weekly

PERSONAL LIST

WORK LIST

Focuses

MY SPIRIT   MY LOVED ONES   MY WORKS

MONDAY

TUESDAY

WEDNESDAY

THURSDAY

FRIDAY

SATURDAY

SUNDAY

Weekly Notes

DREAMS

WHY?

MONEY

TOTAL

DATES:

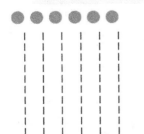

Weekly

PERSONAL LIST

WORK LIST

Focuses

MY SPIRIT   MY LOVED ONES   MY WORKS

MONDAY

TUESDAY

WEDNESDAY

THURSDAY

FRIDAY

SATURDAY

SUNDAY

Weekly Notes

DREAMS

WHY?

MONEY

TOTAL

DATES:

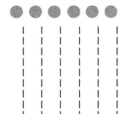

Weekly

PERSONAL LIST

WORK LIST

Focuses

MY SPIRIT

MY LOVED ONES

MY WORKS

MONDAY

TUESDAY

WEDNESDAY

THURSDAY

FRIDAY

SATURDAY

SUNDAY

Weekly Notes

DREAMS

WHY?

MONEY

TOTAL

DATES:

Weekly

PERSONAL LIST

WORK LIST

Focuses

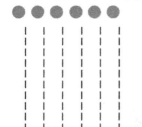

MY SPIRIT

MY LOVED ONES

MY WORKS

MONDAY

TUESDAY

WEDNESDAY

THURSDAY

FRIDAY

SATURDAY

SUNDAY

Weekly Notes

DREAMS

WHY?

MONEY

TOTAL

DATE:

New Moon: To Bestow

INTENTION I

INTENTION II

INTENTION III

I INITIATE/I HATCH:

Full Moon: To Expel

DATE:

NEW MOON INTENTION:

I EVALUATE & FEEL:

INTENTION TO BREAK OR CREATE:

I GIVE:

Dream Reflections

What am I trying to tell myself?

Trends:

Pieces I'm Struck By:

People Involved:

Emotions Experienced:

Archetypes Identified:

Repeated Symbols:

Traditional Meanings:

Personal Meanings Divined Thus Far:

(use the next page to sketch necessary elements)

Tarot Reflections

What am I being told?

Interpretations:

Reflections on Loved Ones

What do I want to remember?

★
★
★
★
★
★
★
★
★
★
★
★
★
★
★
★
★
★

Inner Reflections

What do I think?

What are 3 things that went well?

What were 3 low points?

What did I learn?

Things I'd like to repeat?

Things I want to do differently?

What would I use a wish to change?

When did I feel most alive?

What relationships do I want to improve?

What did I waste time on?

Reflections on Books

What did I read?

Gratitude

What am I thankful for?

_____

_____

_____

_____

_____

_____

_____

_____

_____

_____

_____

_____

_____

_____

_____

_____

_____

_____

_____

_____

June

A Heated Strawberry Moon

THE PLACEMENT OF THE MOON IN CAPRICORN signifies control, discipline, and the part within you that can relate to being a loner. With soulmates Venus and Mars conjunct on the Midheaven, and intensely-focused chthonic ruler Pluto on the Nadir, you may surprise yourself with the amount of charm you muster at this time -- just be sure you're not over-promising.

A Grand Water Trine further begs the controlled emotions to be fully realized and deeply felt -- at least business partnerships and work functions will be favorable.

June

DO NOT FORGET	MONDAY	TUESDAY	WEDNESDAY
		1	2
	7	8	9
	14	15	16
	21	22	23
	28	29	30

Notes

OMENS   BOOKS   SONGS

THURSDAY	FRIDAY	SATURDAY	SUNDAY
3	4	5	6
♊ 10	11	12	13
*solar eclipse 17	18	19	20
♑ 24	25	26	27
27	28	29	30

Works

	PROJECTS	NEW MOON	FULL MOON

DATES: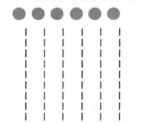

Weekly

PERSONAL LIST	WORK LIST

Focuses

● ● ● ● ● ●

MY SPIRIT

MY LOVED ONES

MY WORKS

MONDAY

TUESDAY

WEDNESDAY

THURSDAY

FRIDAY

SATURDAY

SUNDAY

Weekly Notes

DREAMS	WHY?	MONEY

TOTAL

DATES:

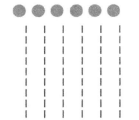

Weekly

PERSONAL LIST

WORK LIST

Focuses

MY SPIRIT   MY LOVED ONES   MY WORKS

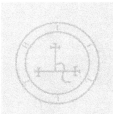

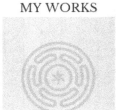

MONDAY

TUESDAY

WEDNESDAY

THURSDAY

FRIDAY

SATURDAY

SUNDAY

Weekly Notes

DREAMS

WHY?

MONEY

TOTAL

DATES:

Weekly

PERSONAL LIST

WORK LIST

Focuses

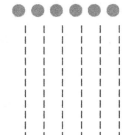

MY SPIRIT

MY LOVED ONES

MY WORKS

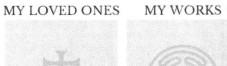

MONDAY

TUESDAY

WEDNESDAY

THURSDAY

FRIDAY

SATURDAY

SUNDAY

Weekly Notes

DREAMS

WHY?

MONEY

TOTAL

DATES:

Weekly

PERSONAL LIST

WORK LIST

Focuses

MY SPIRIT   MY LOVED ONES   MY WORKS

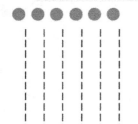

MONDAY

TUESDAY

WEDNESDAY

THURSDAY

FRIDAY

SATURDAY

SUNDAY

Weekly Notes

DREAMS

WHY?

MONEY

TOTAL

DATES:

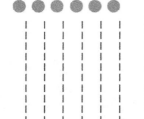

Weekly

PERSONAL LIST

WORK LIST

Focuses

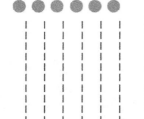

MY SPIRIT

MY LOVED ONES

MY WORKS

MONDAY

TUESDAY

WEDNESDAY

THURSDAY

FRIDAY

SATURDAY

SUNDAY

Weekly Notes

DREAMS

WHY?

MONEY

TOTAL

DATE:

New Moon:
To Bestow

INTENTION I

INTENTION II

INTENTION III

I INITIATE/I HATCH:

Full Moon: To Expel

NEW MOON INTENTION:

I EVALUATE & FEEL:

INTENTION TO BREAK OR CREATE:

I GIVE:

Dream Reflections

What am I trying to tell myself?

Trends:

Pieces I'm Struck By:

People Involved:

Emotions Experienced:

Archetypes Identified:

Repeated Symbols:

Traditional Meanings:

Personal Meanings Divined Thus Far:

(use the next page to sketch necessary elements)

Tarot Reflections

What am I being told?

Interpretations:

Reflections on Loved Ones

What do I want to remember?

★
★
★
★
★
★
★
★
★
★
★
★
★
★
★
★
★
★

Inner Reflections

What do I think?

What are 3 things that went well?

What were 3 low points?

What did I learn?

Things I'd like to repeat?

Things I want to do differently?

What would I use a wish to change?

When did I feel most alive?

What relationships do I want to improve?

What did I waste time on?

Reflections on Books

What did I read?

Gratitude

What am I thankful for?

_____

_____

_____

_____

_____

_____

_____

_____

_____

_____

_____

_____

_____

_____

_____

_____

_____

_____

_____

_____

_____

July

A Weird Wort Moon

THE PLACEMENT OF THE MOON IN AQUARIUS signifies a rebellious, fresh take on emotions during this manic Venus/Mars conjunction on the Midheaven this summer -- a brief respite. Expansive, optimistic Jupiter on the Nadir is a fresh spin on last month's gravity.

Many external planets are in retrograde: Jupiter, Saturn, Neptune, Pluto, even Chiron. Despite a spring full of a reality on the firmament, Neptune's tilted path dips it onto the ascendant to cast an ethereal pall across the stage for the onset of Leo season. These two romantic signs spell trouble unleashed on the Mars/Venus energy conjunction -- a few Yods may facilitate a few karmic opportunities at this time as well.

July

DO NOT FORGET	MONDAY	TUESDAY	WEDNESDAY
	5	6	7
	12	13	14
	19	20	21
	26	27	28

Notes

● ● ● ● ● ●

OMENS	BOOKS	SONGS

THURSDAY	FRIDAY	SATURDAY	SUNDAY
1	2	3	4
8 ♋	9	10	11
15	16	17	18
22 ♒	23	24	25
29	30	31	

Works

● ● ● ● ● ● ●

PROJECTS   NEW MOON   FULL MOON

DATES:

Weekly

PERSONAL LIST

WORK LIST

Focuses

MY SPIRIT

MY LOVED ONES

MY WORKS

MONDAY

TUESDAY

WEDNESDAY

THURSDAY

FRIDAY

SATURDAY

SUNDAY

Weekly Notes

DREAMS

WHY?

MONEY

TOTAL

DATES:

Weekly

PERSONAL LIST

WORK LIST

Focuses

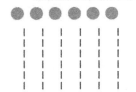

MY SPIRIT

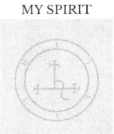

MY LOVED ONES

MY WORKS

MONDAY

TUESDAY

WEDNESDAY

THURSDAY

FRIDAY

SATURDAY

SUNDAY

Weekly Notes

DREAMS

WHY?

MONEY

TOTAL

DATES:

Weekly

PERSONAL LIST

WORK LIST

Focuses

● ● ● ● ● ●

MY SPIRIT 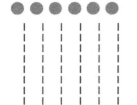   MY LOVED ONES    MY WORKS

MONDAY

TUESDAY

WEDNESDAY

THURSDAY

FRIDAY

SATURDAY

SUNDAY

Weekly Notes

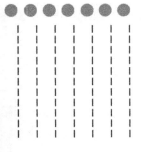

DREAMS	WHY?	MONEY

TOTAL

Weekly

PERSONAL LIST

WORK LIST

Focuses

MY SPIRIT

MY LOVED ONES

MY WORKS

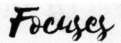

MONDAY

TUESDAY

WEDNESDAY

THURSDAY

FRIDAY

SATURDAY

SUNDAY

Weekly Notes

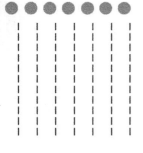

DREAMS

WHY?

MONEY

TOTAL

New Moon: To Bestow

INTENTION I

INTENTION II

INTENTION III

I INITIATE/I HATCH:

Full Moon: To Expel

NEW MOON INTENTION:

I EVALUATE & FEEL:

INTENTION TO BREAK OR CREATE:

I GIVE:

Dream Reflections

What am I trying to tell myself?

Trends:

Pieces I'm Struck By:

People Involved:

Emotions Experienced:

Archetypes Identified:

Repeated Symbols:

Traditional Meanings:

Personal Meanings Divined Thus Far:
               (use the next page to sketch necessary elements)

Tarot Reflections

What am I being told?

Interpretations:

Reflections on Loved Ones

What do I want to remember?

★
★
★
★
★
★
★
★
★
★
★
★
★
★
★
★
★
★
★
★

Inner Reflections

What do I think?

What are 3 things that went well?

What were 3 low points?

What did I learn?

Things I'd like to repeat?

Things I want to do differently?

What would I use a wish to change?

When did I feel most alive?

What relationships do I want to improve?

What did I waste time on?

Reflections on Books

What did I read?

Gratitude

What am I thankful for?

_____

_____

_____

_____

_____

_____

_____

_____

_____

_____

_____

_____

_____

_____

_____

_____

_____

_____

August

A Breezy Fishing Moon

THE PLACEMENT OF THE MOON IN AQUARIUS for the second month in a row signifies a return to friendship as the ideal for the height of summer. Mercury and Mars rising ring in a "me and the boys" energy with jokes spouting like wine. This is also the second Aquarius Moon Opposition Leo Sun energy to up the charisma factor.

External planets are still experiencing retrograde so use this time to enjoy the present, be spontaneous, and go with the flow. There is a Grand Air Trine further underscores the camaraderie and Mutable placements help us remain flexible.

August

	MONDAY	TUESDAY	WEDNESDAY
	2	3	4
	9	10	11
	16	17	18
	23	24	25
	30	31	

Notes

OMENS BOOKS SONGS

THURSDAY	FRIDAY	SATURDAY	SUNDAY
			1
5	6	7 ♌	8
12	13	14	15
19	20	21 ♒	22
26	27	28	29

Works

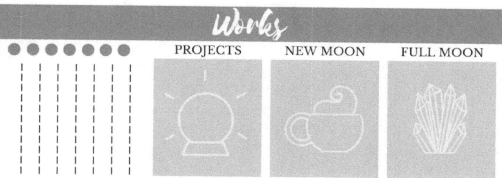

PROJECTS   NEW MOON   FULL MOON

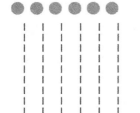

Weekly

PERSONAL LIST

WORK LIST

Focuses

MY SPIRIT   MY LOVED ONES   MY WORKS

MONDAY

TUESDAY

WEDNESDAY

THURSDAY

FRIDAY

SATURDAY

SUNDAY

Weekly Notes

DREAMS

WHY?

MONEY

TOTAL

Weekly

PERSONAL LIST	WORK LIST

Focuses

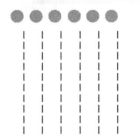

MY SPIRIT

MY LOVED ONES

MY WORKS

MONDAY

TUESDAY

WEDNESDAY

THURSDAY

FRIDAY

SATURDAY

SUNDAY

Weekly Notes

DREAMS   WHY?   MONEY

TOTAL

DATES:

Weekly

PERSONAL LIST

WORK LIST

Focuses

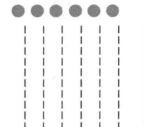

MY SPIRIT

MY LOVED ONES

MY WORKS

MONDAY

TUESDAY

WEDNESDAY

THURSDAY

FRIDAY

SATURDAY

SUNDAY

Weekly Notes

DREAMS

WHY?

MONEY

TOTAL

DATES:

Weekly

PERSONAL LIST

WORK LIST

Focuses

MY SPIRIT  MY LOVED ONES  MY WORKS

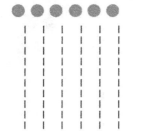

MONDAY

TUESDAY

WEDNESDAY

THURSDAY

FRIDAY

SATURDAY

SUNDAY

Weekly Notes

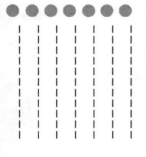

DREAMS

WHY?

MONEY

TOTAL

DATES:

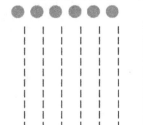

Weekly

PERSONAL LIST	WORK LIST

Focuses

MY SPIRIT MY LOVED ONES MY WORKS

MONDAY

TUESDAY

WEDNESDAY

THURSDAY

FRIDAY

SATURDAY

SUNDAY

Weekly Notes

DREAMS

WHY?

MONEY

TOTAL

New Moon: To Bestow

INTENTION I

INTENTION II

INTENTION III

I INITIATE/I HATCH:

Full Moon: To Expel

NEW MOON INTENTION:

I EVALUATE & FEEL:

INTENTION TO BREAK OR CREATE:

I GIVE:

Dream Reflections

What am I trying to tell myself?

Trends:

Pieces I'm Struck By:

People Involved:

Emotions Experienced:

Archetypes Identified:

Repeated Symbols:

Traditional Meanings:

Personal Meanings Divined Thus Far:

(use the next page to sketch necessary elements)

Tarot Reflections

What am I being told?

Interpretations:

Reflections on Loved Ones

What do I want to remember?

★
★
★
★
★
★
★
★
★
★
★
★
★
★
★
★
★
★
★
★

Inner Reflections

What do I think?

What are 3 things that went well?

What were 3 low points?

What did I learn?

Things I'd like to repeat?

Things I want to do differently?

What would I use a wish to change?

When did I feel most alive?

What relationships do I want to improve?

What did I waste time on?

Reflections on Books

What did I read?

Gratitude

What am I thankful for?

September

A Psychic Autumnal Equinox

THE PLACEMENT OF THE MOON IN PISCES signifies an emotional swelling with emphasis on the intuitive and psychic strengths: with the Sun in Virgo, sensitive Pisces softens the sharp edges of this on-edge, exacting season, ready to slip into Libra season and rest after a harvest season of hard work.

A Grand Air Trine with the absence of any inner planetary placements in a fire sign helps us do the hard work of discussing our deeply felt emotions without rushing into the next task, as Capricorn rising has been begging us for the last little while. Venus in fellow water sign Scorpio on the Midheaven may bring a little romance into your life.

September

1

♍ 6 7 8

13 14 15

♓ 20 21 22

27 28 29

Notes

OMENS   BOOKS   SONGS

THURSDAY	FRIDAY	SATURDAY	SUNDAY
2	3	4	5
9	10	11	12
16	17	18	19
23	24	25	26
30			

Works

● ● ● ● ● ● ●

PROJECTS	NEW MOON	FULL MOON

DATES:

Weekly

PERSONAL LIST

WORK LIST

Focuses

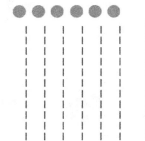

MY SPIRIT	MY LOVED ONES	MY WORKS

MONDAY

TUESDAY

WEDNESDAY

THURSDAY

FRIDAY

SATURDAY

SUNDAY

Weekly Notes

DREAMS

WHY?

MONEY

TOTAL

DATES:

Weekly

PERSONAL LIST

WORK LIST

Focuses

MY SPIRIT MY LOVED ONES MY WORKS

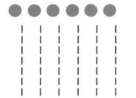

MONDAY

TUESDAY

WEDNESDAY

THURSDAY

FRIDAY

SATURDAY

SUNDAY

Weekly Notes

DREAMS

WHY?

MONEY

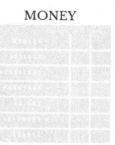

TOTAL

DATES:

Weekly

PERSONAL LIST

WORK LIST

Focuses

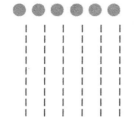

MY SPIRIT

MY LOVED ONES

MY WORKS

MONDAY

TUESDAY

WEDNESDAY

THURSDAY

FRIDAY

SATURDAY

SUNDAY

Weekly Notes

DREAMS

WHY?

MONEY

TOTAL

DATES:

Weekly

PERSONAL LIST

WORK LIST

Focuses

MY SPIRIT   MY LOVED ONES   MY WORKS

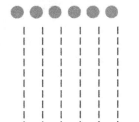   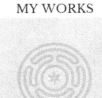

MONDAY

TUESDAY

WEDNESDAY

THURSDAY

FRIDAY

SATURDAY

SUNDAY

Weekly Notes

DREAMS

WHY?

MONEY

TOTAL

DATE:

New Moon:
To Bestow

INTENTION I

INTENTION II

INTENTION III

I INITIATE/I HATCH:

Full Moon: To Expel

NEW MOON INTENTION:

I EVALUATE & FEEL:

INTENTION TO BREAK OR CREATE:

I GIVE:

Dream Reflections

What am I trying to tell myself?

Trends:

Pieces I'm Struck By:

People Involved:

Emotions Experienced:

Archetypes Identified:

Repeated Symbols:

Traditional Meanings:

Personal Meanings Divined Thus Far:

(use the next page to sketch necessary elements)

Tarot Reflections

What am I being told?

Interpretations:

Reflections on Loved Ones

What do I want to remember?

★
★
★
★
★
★
★
★
★
★
★
★
★
★
★
★
★
★
★

Inner Reflections

What do I think?

What are 3 things that went well?

What were 3 low points?

What did I learn?

Things I'd like to repeat?

Things I want to do differently?

What would I use a wish to change?

When did I feel most alive?

What relationships do I want to improve?

What did I waste time on?

Reflections on Books

What did I read?

Gratitude

What am I thankful for?

_____
_____
_____
_____
_____
_____
_____
_____
_____
_____
_____
_____
_____
_____
_____
_____
_____
_____
_____
_____

October

A Horned Sanguine Moon

THE PLACEMENT OF THE MOON IN ARIES signifies an devilish, assertive, and impulsive emotional energy. The Libra Sun is in its final hours and the childlike Ram insists you pay attention to your passions: Saturn is rising with the North Node on the Nadir -- a recipe for re-focusing on your "life's work" and your responsibility to yourself.

Venus in wild and free Sagittarius forms aspects with a multitude of bodies, with the dominant Air element of the inner planets fanning the flames. Just remember that the inner planets do not *even once* fall in a balancing Water or Earth sign so proceed at your own risk.

October

DO NOT FORGET	MONDAY	TUESDAY	WEDNESDAY
		4	5 ♎	6
	11	12	13
	18	19 ♈	20
	25	26	27

Notes

● ● ● ● ● ●

OMENS	BOOKS	SONGS

THURSDAY	FRIDAY	SATURDAY	SUNDAY
	1	2	3
7	8	9	10
14	15	16	17
21	22	23	24
28	29	30	31

Works

	PROJECTS	NEW MOON	FULL MOON

DATES:

Weekly

PERSONAL LIST

WORK LIST

Focuses

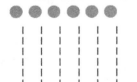

MY SPIRIT

MY LOVED ONES

MY WORKS

MONDAY

TUESDAY

WEDNESDAY

THURSDAY

FRIDAY

SATURDAY

SUNDAY

Weekly Notes

DREAMS

WHY?

MONEY

TOTAL

Weekly

PERSONAL LIST

WORK LIST

Focuses

MY SPIRIT **MY LOVED ONES** **MY WORKS**

MONDAY

TUESDAY

WEDNESDAY

THURSDAY

FRIDAY

SATURDAY

SUNDAY

Weekly Notes

DREAMS

WHY?

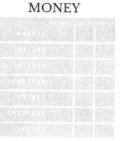

MONEY

TOTAL

Weekly

PERSONAL LIST

WORK LIST

Focuses

MY SPIRIT   MY LOVED ONES   MY WORKS

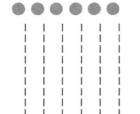

MONDAY

TUESDAY

WEDNESDAY

THURSDAY

FRIDAY

SATURDAY

SUNDAY

Weekly Notes

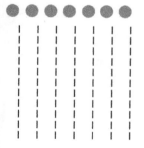

DREAMS

WHY?

MONEY

TOTAL

DATES:

Weekly

PERSONAL LIST

WORK LIST

Focuses

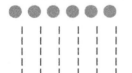

MY SPIRIT

MY LOVED ONES

MY WORKS

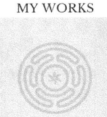

MONDAY

TUESDAY

WEDNESDAY

THURSDAY

FRIDAY

SATURDAY

SUNDAY

Weekly Notes

DREAMS	WHY?	MONEY

TOTAL

DATES: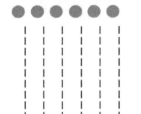

Weekly

PERSONAL LIST	WORK LIST

Focuses

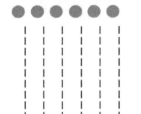

MY SPIRIT	MY LOVED ONES	MY WORKS

MONDAY

TUESDAY

WEDNESDAY

THURSDAY

FRIDAY

SATURDAY

SUNDAY

Weekly Notes

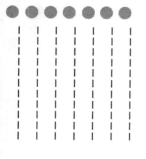

DREAMS

WHY?

MONEY

TOTAL

New Moon:
To Bestow

INTENTION I

INTENTION II

INTENTION III

I INITIATE/I HATCH:

Full Moon: To Expel

NEW MOON INTENTION:

I EVALUATE & FEEL:

INTENTION TO BREAK OR CREATE:

I GIVE:

Dream Reflections

What am I trying to tell myself?

Trends:

Pieces I'm Struck By:

People Involved:

Emotions Experienced:

Archetypes Identified:

Repeated Symbols:

Traditional Meanings:

Personal Meanings Divined Thus Far:
  (use the next page to sketch necessary elements)

Tarot Reflections

What am I being told?

Interpretations:

Reflections on Loved Ones

What do I want to remember?

★
★
★
★
★
★
★
★
★
★
★
★
★
★
★
★
★
★
★

Inner Reflections

What do I think?

What are 3 things that went well?

What were 3 low points?

What did I learn?

Things I'd like to repeat?

Things I want to do differently?

What would I use a wish to change?

When did I feel most alive?

What relationships do I want to improve?

What did I waste time on?

Reflections on Books

What did I read?

Gratitude

What am I thankful for?

_____
_____
_____
_____
_____
_____
_____
_____
_____
_____
_____
_____
_____
_____
_____
_____
_____
_____
_____

November

A Frosty Blood Moon

THE PLACEMENT OF THE MOON IN GEMINI signifies a frenetic transition from fall into winter and the very end of the year. The bottom right quadrant of this Moon's chart is empty, signifying a pulling away from loved ones or our current environment. Venus remains on the Midheaven, keeping your passions on your mind, although with its placement in Capricorn it likely isn't the romantic interlude you're hoping for.

The Sun, Mercury, and Mars are conjunct in Scorpio, with Jupiter and Saturn out of retrograde -- expect an intense, somewhat vexing vibe to permeate pre-holiday affairs.

November

DO NOT FORGET	MONDAY	TUESDAY	WEDNESDAY
	1	2	3
	8	9	10
	15	16	17
	22	23	24
	29	30	

Notes

OMENS

BOOKS

SONGS

THURSDAY	FRIDAY	SATURDAY	SUNDAY
♏ 4	5	6	7
11	12	13	14
18 ♊	19	20	21
	lunar eclipse		
25	26	27	28

Works

PROJECTS	NEW MOON	FULL MOON

DATES:

Weekly

PERSONAL LIST

WORK LIST

Focuses

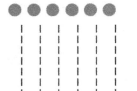

MY SPIRIT

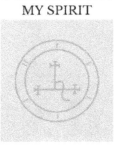

MY LOVED ONES

MY WORKS

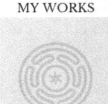

MONDAY

TUESDAY

WEDNESDAY

THURSDAY

FRIDAY

SATURDAY

SUNDAY

Weekly Notes

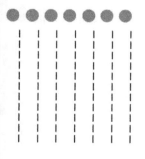

DREAMS

WHY?

MONEY

TOTAL

DATES: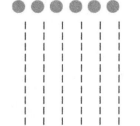

Weekly

PERSONAL LIST

WORK LIST

Focuses

MY SPIRIT   MY LOVED ONES   MY WORKS

MONDAY

TUESDAY

WEDNESDAY

THURSDAY

FRIDAY

SATURDAY

SUNDAY

Weekly Notes

DREAMS

WHY?

MONEY

TOTAL

Weekly

PERSONAL LIST

WORK LIST

Focuses

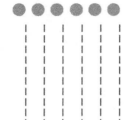

MY SPIRIT

MY LOVED ONES

MY WORKS

MONDAY

TUESDAY

WEDNESDAY

THURSDAY

FRIDAY

SATURDAY

SUNDAY

Weekly Notes

DREAMS

WHY?

MONEY

TOTAL

DATES:

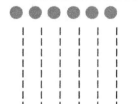

Weekly

PERSONAL LIST

WORK LIST

Focuses

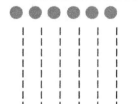

MY SPIRIT

MY LOVED ONES

MY WORKS

MONDAY

TUESDAY

WEDNESDAY

THURSDAY

FRIDAY

SATURDAY

SUNDAY

Weekly Notes

DREAMS	WHY?	MONEY

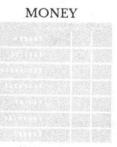

TOTAL

DATES:

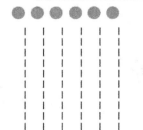

Weekly

PERSONAL LIST

WORK LIST

Focuses

MY SPIRIT   MY LOVED ONES   MY WORKS

MONDAY

TUESDAY

WEDNESDAY

THURSDAY

FRIDAY

SATURDAY

SUNDAY

Weekly Notes

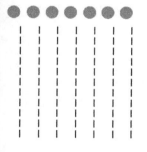

DREAMS

WHY?

MONEY

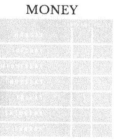

TOTAL

DATE:

New Moon:
To Bestow

INTENTION I

INTENTION II

INTENTION III

I INITIATE/I HATCH:

Full Moon: To Expel

NEW MOON INTENTION:

I EVALUATE & FEEL:

INTENTION TO BREAK OR CREATE:

I GIVE:

Dream Reflections

What am I trying to tell myself?

Trends:

Pieces I'm Struck By:

People Involved:

Emotions Experienced:

Archetypes Identified:

Repeated Symbols:

Traditional Meanings:

Personal Meanings Divined Thus Far:

(use the next page to sketch necessary elements)

Tarot Reflections

What am I being told?

Interpretations:

Reflections on Loved Ones

What do I want to remember?

★
★
★
★
★
★
★
★
★
★
★
★
★
★
★
★
★
★

Inner Reflections

What do I think?

What are 3 things that went well?

What were 3 low points?

What did I learn?

Things I'd like to repeat?

Things I want to do differently?

What would I use a wish to change?

When did I feel most alive?

What relationships do I want to improve?

What did I waste time on?

Reflections on Books

What did I read?

Gratitude

What am I thankful for?

_____

_____

_____

_____

_____

_____

_____

_____

_____

_____

_____

_____

_____

_____

_____

_____

_____

_____

_____

_____

December

A Cold, Mingling Moon

THE PLACEMENT OF THE MOON IN GEMINI signifies the excitement of hair-brained schemes when in conjunction with the Sagittarius Sun and Jupiter and Saturn in Uranus. This time is not without its obstacles (Square aspects) but flexible Gemini and Sagittarius can jump the hurdles.

It's not all fun-and-games with Mercury (communication) and Venus (passion/love) in staunch, steadfast Capricorn, but with Gemini rising casting the warm glow of camaraderie during lucky Sagittarius Season. The Air element and Mutable energy is dominant and the North Node is also rising -- time to get out there and network, talking to friends and business prospects about your life's work and what your occupational plans are for the coming year!

December

DO NOT FORGET	MONDAY	TUESDAY	WEDNESDAY
			1
	6	7	8
	13	14	15
	20	21	22
	27	28	29

Notes

● ● ● ● ● ●

OMENS

BOOKS

SONGS

new moon: 12/4 🏹   full moon: 12/18 ♊

THURSDAY	FRIDAY	SATURDAY	SUNDAY
2	3 🏹	4	5
		solar eclipse	
9	10	11	12
16	17 ♊	18	19
23	24	25	26
30	31		

Works

● ● ● ● ● ● ●

PROJECTS   NEW MOON   FULL MOON

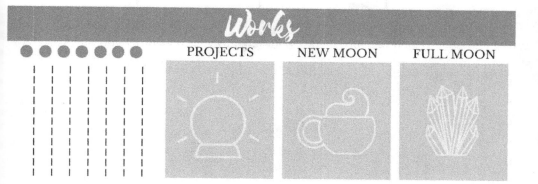

DATES:

Weekly

PERSONAL LIST	WORK LIST

Focuses

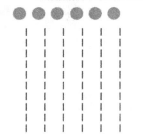

MY SPIRIT

MY LOVED ONES   MY WORKS

MONDAY

TUESDAY

WEDNESDAY

THURSDAY

FRIDAY

SATURDAY

SUNDAY

Weekly Notes

DREAMS

WHY?

MONEY

TOTAL

DATES:

Weekly

PERSONAL LIST

WORK LIST

Focuses

MY SPIRIT  MY LOVED ONES  MY WORKS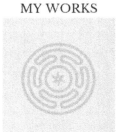

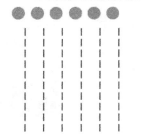

MONDAY

TUESDAY

WEDNESDAY

THURSDAY

FRIDAY

SATURDAY

SUNDAY

Weekly Notes

DREAMS

WHY?

MONEY

TOTAL

DATES:

Weekly

PERSONAL LIST

WORK LIST

Focuses

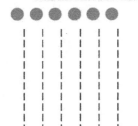
MY SPIRIT

MY LOVED ONES

MY WORKS

MONDAY

TUESDAY

WEDNESDAY

THURSDAY

FRIDAY

SATURDAY

SUNDAY

Weekly Notes

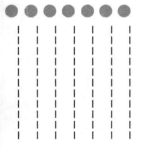

DREAMS	WHY?	MONEY

TOTAL

DATES:

Weekly

PERSONAL LIST

WORK LIST

Focuses

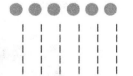

MY SPIRIT   MY LOVED ONES   MY WORKS

MONDAY

TUESDAY

WEDNESDAY

THURSDAY

FRIDAY

SATURDAY

SUNDAY

Weekly Notes

DREAMS

WHY?

MONEY

TOTAL

Weekly

PERSONAL LIST

WORK LIST

Focuses

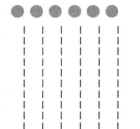

MY SPIRIT

MY LOVED ONES

MY WORKS

MONDAY

TUESDAY

WEDNESDAY

THURSDAY

FRIDAY

SATURDAY

SUNDAY

Weekly Notes

DREAMS

WHY?

MONEY

TOTAL

DATE:

New Moon: To Bestow

INTENTION I

INTENTION II

INTENTION III

I INITIATE/I HATCH:

NEW MOON INTENTION:

I EVALUATE & FEEL:

INTENTION TO BREAK OR CREATE:

I GIVE:

Reflections on Loved Ones

What do I want to remember?

★
★
★
★
★
★
★
★
★
★
★
★
★
★
★
★
★
★

Inner Reflections

What do I think?

What are 3 things that went well?

What were 3 low points?

What did I learn?

Things I'd like to repeat?

Things I want to do differently?

What would I use a wish to change?

When did I feel most alive?

What relationships do I want to improve?

What did I waste time on?

Reflections on Books

What did I read?

_____
_____
_____
_____
_____
_____
_____
_____
_____
_____
_____
_____
_____
_____
_____
_____
_____
_____
_____

Gratitude

What am I thankful for?

_____

_____

_____

_____

_____

_____

_____

_____

_____

_____

_____

_____

_____

_____

_____

_____

_____

_____

2021 Denouement

You've Made it: What did you think?

I am most grateful for:

I quit:

I started

I was totally transformed by:

My dreams came true when:

I sold:

I was given:

I gave away:

I grew:

I let go of:

I made friends with:

I've conjured up the dream to:

I never thought I'd:

I created:

I learnt how to:

I'm so incredibly proud of:

I was inspired by:

I was surprised by:

I shed tears when:

I remembered:

I laughed the hardest at:

I travelled to:

I still can't believe I overcame:

I will never forget when:

The biggest lesson I learned was:

Acknowledgments

Thank you to my husband, Chris, for listening to my endless rants and being on the same weird playing field as I am; thank you to my sister, Lexx who, though busy with her own plate full of projects, is always available to bounce ideas off of; thank you to my nerdy friend-family, chiefly among them, Dani, for helping me remember that there's more to life than work; lastly thank you to Aunt Laurie, for introducing me to the world of publishing, starting me down the path of the weird, and showing me that High Strangeness is rarely ever bad.

About the Author

Nico Harlakenden is an Author, Graphic Designer, and student of the stars. She owns Newton Press, a small independent publishing company.

Nico lived a creatively and academically promising childhood and adolescence then took a few years off to travel and live the gritty kind of life certain writer-types idealize. She spent many years studying language, ancient and modern myths, history, the paranormal, and the occult. From homeroom to hostels, homeless to home again, Nico is grateful for the rich tapestry of experiences she's been afforded and for most of the souls she's met along the way.

In her spare time she listens to a variety of music, watches horror and science fiction films, and ventures into the wilderness -- happy to return to a hot cup of tea. She and her husband, Christopher, currently live in the wooded paradise that is Maine with their two dogs, Yoko and Tepe.

www.thenewtonpress.com

Thanks for reading! Please add a short review on Amazon and let us know what you thought.

Coming 2021:

Book 1 of the Cetus Trilogy:
Cup-Bearer, Sword-Bearer

For more titles by Nico Harlakenden and like authors, visit www.thenewtonpress.com

CPSIA information can be obtained
at www.ICGtesting.com
Printed in the USA
LVHW081024181020
669074LV00046B/1302/J